BIBLE BASICS

for
Spirit-filled
Believers

by
LEON BIBLE

MINISTRY HELPS
Laurens, South Carolina

2002

BIBLE BASICS
for Spirit-filled Believers
"a study guide for those who follow Christ"

by Leon Bible

Published by: **MINISTRY HELPS**
746 Vern-Cora Road
Laurens, South Carolina 29360
Telephone: (864) 682-5425 • Fax: (864) 682-5428
Website: http://www.ministryhelps.com

Bookstores obtain from:

Dake Publishing, Inc.
P.O. Box 1050
Lawrenceville, Georgia 30046-1050
1 (800) 241-1239

First Printing 1999
Second Printing 2002

Printed in the United States of America.

Recommended Dewey Decimal Classification: 248
Suggested Subject Heading: CHRISTIAN LIVING

Library of Congress Catalog Card Number: 97-90752

ISBN: 0-9671995-1-4 (paperback)

All scripture taken from the *Holy Bible, King James Version.*

For more information or to order additional copies of this study guide, or other books,
contact the author at the address above. This study guide is available at a considerable
discount when purchased in quantity.

Contents

Introduction

This study guide on Bible basics is intended to be just that. It is not a comprehensive study dealing with every thing the believer needs to know in his or her Christian walk. The purpose of this guide is to deal with the essentials that are needed most.

In this guide you will notice that very little comment is given. The Bible is a living book, and it is my intention to let the Bible speak for itself.

This guide is written so that it can be used many different ways: as a personal Bible study; a group Bible study; or a Bible study taught by the Pastor or leaders in the local church.

This Bible study is as the title suggest Spirit-filled. That is, the Word of God is inspired by the Holy Spirit, and it is also accepted that based on the teaching of the Bible, that the Spirit-filled experience is available for believing Christians today.

While this guide emphasizes the power of the Holy Spirit through out, it does not venture into fringe areas or experiences which are not found within the pages of the Bible.

Now a little bit about the layout of this guide. The guide is laid out in outline form. By reading the titles of each division and then the subtitles as well as the accompanying Scripture, a plain and simply Bible lesson can be taught and understood. The questions that are given after each verse of Scripture are for extra emphasis and meditation of the point that the Scripture has made. No thought or statement is made that is not clearly a teaching of the particular Scripture cited.

At the conclusion of each chapter is a box entitled assignments. These assignments are to encourage you in the following ways: To read the entire New Testament through in the time that it takes to complete this guide. Twelve weeks is suggested. A memory verse is given which embodies the greatest overall thought of the chapter just studied. In the back of the book you will find "cut out" memory verses to aid you in memorizing the Scriptures. A suggestion as to applying the word into your life each day is given in the Speak the Word section. Also, suggestions for applying the lessons in your prayer time are given.

In addition to the assignments at the end of each chapter, you will also find a Journal or Notes sheet. This space is provided for note taking when you are in a class type setting. If you are studying this guide alone, you may use this as your personal journal to record any ideas and revelation you receive.

In the back of the book you will find a progress sheet, which will help you keep track as you work your way through this study guide.

It is the author's prayer that this guide helps everyone who uses it to become more Christ-like in every way. Indeed, faithful commitment to the completion of this guide and to the principles which it teaches will accomplish this goal.

Author's Dedication

I dedicate this book to My Dad.
It was my Dad who first told me of God's love for me.
He always told me that I could go to the Word of God
to find all the answers to life's questions.
He was right.

The New Birth

I confess with my mouth
that Jesus is Lord,
I believe in my heart
that God has raised Him
from the dead,
therefore I am saved,
I am a child of God,
I am born again.

The New Birth

Introduction: What The New Birth Experience Is Not

Confirmation	Church membership	Water Baptism
Card signing	Taking the Sacrament	Shaking the Pastor's hand
Saying prayers	Memorizing creeds	Being morally good
Going to church	Reading the Bible	Doing good deeds
Religious duties	Intellectual reception	Being cultured or refined

As good as some of the above may be, not one of these constitutes the New Birth experience of being Born Again.

In this chapter on the New Birth we will study the truth of God's Word about salvation. Contained within the pages of the Bible is everything we need to know in order to understand and experience the power of the New Birth.

Read John 20:30-31 from your Bible.

Why was the Word of God written? (verse 31)

___

What The New Birth Is

1. The New Birth is the act of being made a child of God.

Read John 1:6-13 from your Bible.

What is our new relationship with God? (verse 12)

___

2. The New Birth is having our sins forgiven.

Read 1 John 1:8-10 from your Bible.

What must we do in order to have our sins forgiven? (verse 9)

___

When we confess our sins what does God promise to do?

___

3. The New Birth is being made a new creation.

Read 2 Corinthians 5:14-21 from your Bible.

Bible Basics for Spirit-filled Believers

If a man is in Christ Jesus, what is he? (verse 17)

_____

4. The New Birth is receiving peace from God.

Read Romans 5:1-5 from your Bible.

Who does our peace with God come through? (verse 1)

_____

5. The New Birth is having fellowship with God.

Read 1 John 1:3-7 from your Bible.

Name three persons we now have fellowship with. (verse 3)

_____

The New Birth Is Absolutely Necessary

1. Jesus told Nicodemus that he must be born again.

Read John 3:3 from your Bible.

What must happen to a man before he can see the Kingdom of God?

_____

2. A conversion must take place.

Read Matthew 18:1-5 from your Bible.

For one to enter the Kingdom of Heaven what must happen? (verse 3)

_____

3. Without repentance all will perish.

Read Luke 13:1-5 from your Bible.

What must we do in order not to perish? (verse 3 and 5)

_____

The New Birth

Five Steps To Take In Order To Be Born Again

Step 1 - Realize that we are a sinner.

Read Romans 3:21-26 from your Bible.

Is there anyone who has not sinned? (verse 23)

Step 2 - Realize sin has a penalty.

Read Romans 6:15-23 from your Bible.

What is the wages of sin? (verse 23)

Step 3 - Realize God loves us and has already paid our sin penalty.

Read Romans 5:6-11 from your Bible.

At what time in our lives did God love us? (verse 8)

Step 4 - Realize we receive salvation as a gift.

Read Romans 6:15-23 from your Bible.

What is eternal life called in this verse? (verse 23)

Step 5 - Receive salvation now.

Read Romans 10:9-13 from your Bible.

What two things are we told to do? What promise is made? (verse 10)

Bible Basics for Spirit-filled Believers

We can be born again by simply believing on Christ as God's Son and confessing Him as our Lord and Savior. If you have never prayed to receive Christ as Lord and Savior, then right now, pray the following prayer in faith believing and Christ will come into your life.

A Prayer For Salvation

Dear God,
Be merciful to me a sinner!
Forgive me of all my sins and blot out my transgressions.
Cleanse me from all unrighteousness and make me clean by the precious blood of Jesus Christ and by the power of the Holy Spirit.
I will forsake sin and consecrate my life to your service and to the good of others and walk in the light of your Word; the Bible.
I now believe, that you forgive me and according to your Word in *Romans 10:9-10*, I am saved.
I am Born Again.
In Jesus' name I ask and believe.
Thank You my Father.
AMEN!

Chapter 1 Assignments

❏ **Bible Reading**

Read Chapters 1-21 in the book of Matthew

❏ **Memory Verse**

Romans 10:9 That if thou shalt confess with thy mouth the Lord Jesus, and shalt believe in thine heart that God hath raised him from the dead, thou shalt be saved.

10 For with the heart man believeth unto righteousness; and with the mouth confession is made unto salvation

❏ **Speak The Word**

I confess with my mouth that Jesus is my Lord, therefore I am saved, I am a child of God, I am born again.

❏ **Prayer Time**

Begin to set aside time each day for prayer. Talk to God just as you would a close friend. Right now, do two things. 1) Set a time to pray, and 2) select a place to pray. All relationships must have communication. For your relationship with God to be complete, you must make prayer a top priority in your life.

The New Birth

Journal/Notes

_____
_____
_____
_____
_____
_____
_____
_____
_____
_____
_____
_____
_____
_____
_____
_____
_____
_____
_____
_____
_____
_____
_____
_____

Discipleship

I continue in God's
Word, therefore,
I am a disciple
of the Lord.

Discipleship

Introduction

A disciple is a student, a learner, and a pupil. In the Bible the word is used most often to refer to a follower of Jesus Christ. Now that you have received Jesus Christ as your Lord, you have become a disciple. As a disciple you will begin to live your life just as Jesus lived His life.

Read Matthew 28:16-20 from your Bible.

What are disciples to observe? (verse 20)

_____

What A Disciple Is

1. A Disciple is a believer.

Read Acts 16:16-34 from your Bible.

What was the jailer told he must do to be saved? (verse 31)

_____

2. A Disciple is a follower.

Read Matthew 16:24-27 from your Bible.

What are the three things that disciples do to follow Jesus? (verse 24)

_____

3. A Disciple is a learner.

Read John 8:31-36 from your Bible.

As a disciple, what are we to learn? (verse 32)

_____

4. A Disciple is a witness.

Read 1 Peter 3:13-17 from your Bible.

How will learning the Word of God help you to be a witness? (verse 15)

_____

Bible Basics for Spirit-filled Believers

Six Things Jesus Said About A Disciple

1. Jesus said a Disciple is one who abides in Him.

Read John 15:1-8 from your Bible.

Who are we to abide in and what is to abide in us? (verse 7)

_____

Then what promise do we have? (verse 7)

_____

Read 2 Timothy 2:14-19 from your Bible.

What should we do to cause the Word to abide in us? (verse 15)

_____

Read Romans 12:1-2 from your Bible.

How is the mind of man to be renewed and transformed?

_____

2. Jesus said a Disciple is obedient.

Read John 15:9-14 from your Bible.

How does Jesus say we are to abide in his love? (verse 10)

_____

3. Jesus said a Disciple bears fruit.

Read John 15:15-17 from your Bible.

What do you think is the greatest kind of fruit we can bear? (verse 17)

_____

Read Galatians 5:16-26 from your Bible.

Think about how the fruit of the Spirit is needed in your life.

14

Discipleship

4. Jesus said a Disciple glorifies God.

Read John 15:1-8 from your Bible.

What brings glory to God? (verse 8)

_____

Read John 14:12-14 from your Bible.

When is the Father glorified in the Son?

_____

5. Jesus said a Disciple manifest joy in his life.

Read John 15:9-11 from your Bible.

What does listening to the Words of Jesus do for disciples? (verse 11)

_____

Read Hebrews 12:1-2 from your Bible.

In difficult times what is needed to endure to the end?

_____

6. Jesus said a Disciple loves as He himself loves.

Read John 15:12-14 from your Bible.

As disciples of Christ, how are we to love? (verse 12)

_____

Read 1 Corinthians 13:4-7 from your Bible.

List as many of the characteristics of the God kind of love as you can.

_____

_____

_____

Bible Basics for Spirit-filled Believers

The Road To Discipleship Is A Road To Victory

In the rest of this study guide you will continue on the road to discipleship. You will learn the doctrine of a disciple, how to pray, how to worship, how to witness, how to be healed, how to receive the power of the Spirit and so much more. Do not let anything keep you from giving your all through discipleship to our Lord Jesus Christ.

Make a vow now to God, that nothing will hinder you. God loves you and wants to bring many blessings into your life. The truths that you will learn in this study guide will enable you to be blessed and be a blessing to your family and others who are in need of God's love.

May God bless you as you continue on the road to victory!

Chapter 2 Assignments

❑ **Bible Reading**

Read chapters 22 - 28 in the book of Matthew, and chapters 1 - 16 in the book of Mark.

❑ **Memory Verse**

John 8:31 Then said Jesus to those Jews which believed on him, If ye continue in my word, then are ye my disciples indeed;

❑ **Speak The Word**

I continue in God's Word, therefore, I am a disciple of the Lord.

❑ **Prayer Time**

As you continue your prayer life this week, dedicate yourself to the Lord as one of His disciples. Covenant with the Lord to give Him your very best in every area of your life.

Discipleship

Journal/Notes

_____

_____

_____

_____

_____

_____

_____

_____

_____

_____

_____

_____

_____

_____

_____

_____

_____

_____

_____

_____

_____

_____

_____

The Bible

I am throughly furnished unto all good works, by the power of God's Word.

The Bible

Introduction

As a child of God you should read the Bible every day. The Bible is food for your Spiritual life. It is a revelation of God's instructions to mankind. The Bible is a library of 66 books revealing God's plan for man. It was written over a period of 1,500 years by more than 40 writers. Although many years and many writers were involved, the unity of the Bible is nothing less than a miracle. It is God's Word.

This chapter is devoted to understanding just what the Bible is and what it means in the life of the believer.

Bible Basics

Turn to the contents page in the front of your Bible and answer the following questions.

What are the two divisions of the Bible?

_____ and _____

How many books are in the Old Testament?   _____

How many books are in the New Testament?   _____

How To Understand And Receive The Bible

To understand the Bible, ask these five questions.

1. Meaning - What does this passage say?
2. Promises - Does this passage contain a promise I may claim?
3. Warnings - Are there any warnings in this passage?
4. Commands - Is this passage a command that I must take heed to?
5. Parallels - Are there any other similar verses in the Bible that would shed light on the understanding of this passage?

To receive the Bible, use these five keys.

1. Read and study the Bible.

Read Acts 17:10-14 from your Bible.

What two things did the Bereans do concerning the Word? (verse 11)

_____

Bible Basics for Spirit-filled Believers

2. Memorize the Bible.

Read Romans 10:8 from your Bible.

What two places should the Word of God be in us?

_____

3. Meditate (think on or mutter) the Bible.

Read Joshua 1:1-9 from your Bible.

What happens when we meditate and do the Word of God? (verse 8)

_____

4. Believe or mix faith with the Bible.

Read Hebrews 4:1-2 from your Bible.

Why did not the Word of God profit these people? (verse 2)

_____

5. Rely on the Holy Spirit to give you revelation.

Read 1 Corinthians 2:6-16 from your Bible.

Who does this verse say is the teacher of the Bible? (verse 13)

_____

The Bible Is God's Word To Mankind

Read 2 Timothy 3:10-17 from your Bible.

Who has given us our Bible? (verse 16)

_____

Read 2 Peter 1:16-21 from your Bible.

Who moved upon men to speak the words of the Bible? (verse 21)

_____

The Bible

Reasons Why The Bible Is True

1. God the author of the Bible is not a liar.

Read Numbers 23:19 from your Bible.

Men may lie, but is God like a man and does He ever lie?

_____

2. The transforming power of the Bible in the lives of believers.

Read 2 Corinthians 5:14-21 from your Bible.

Can you testify that the Bible has made a change in you? (verse 17)

_____

The Purpose Of The Bible

1. The Bible reveals God's plan for our lives.

Read John 3:16 from your Bible.

In your own words write down what this verse means to you personally.

_____

2. The Bible gives us direction on how to live our lives.

Read Psalms 119:105-112 from your Bible.

What two things is the Bible called? (verse 105)

_____

_____

3. The Bible gives us God's commandments.

Read Exodus 20:1-17 from your Bible.

How many commandments are included in these verses?

_____

Bible Basics for Spirit-filled Believers

Blessings The Bible Brings

Look up and read each verse of scripture following the principles below.

1. The Bible gives faith. *Romans 10:14-17*

2. The Bible gives a spiritual bath and victory over sin. *Psalms 119:9-16*

3. The Bible gives life to the spirit. *John 6:60-63*

4. The Bible gives health to the body. *Proverbs 4:20-27*

5. The Bible gives spiritual food. *Matthew 4:1-4*

6. The Bible gives the power of God. *Romans 1:16-17*

7. The Bible gives a weapon to fight the enemy with. *Ephesians 6:10-20*

Chapter 3 Assignments

❑ **Bible Reading**

Read chapters 1 - 24 in the book of Luke, and chapters 1 - 3 in the book of John.

❑ **Memory Verse**

2 Timothy 3:16 All scripture is given by inspiration of God, and is profitable for doctrine, for reproof, for correction, for instruction in righteousness:

17 That the man of God may be perfect, throughly furnished unto all good works.

❑ **Speak The Word**

I am throughly furnished unto all good works, by the power of God's Word.

❑ **Prayer Time**

During your prayer time this week, ask God to help you establish and discipline your life to include a regular plan of Bible reading and study. Ask God to let His Word become your word. As you pray, remind God of His promises, and lay hold to them by faith.

The Bible

Journal/Notes

_____

_____

_____

_____

_____

_____

_____

_____

_____

_____

_____

_____

_____

_____

_____

_____

_____

_____

_____

_____

_____

_____

_____

_____

Bible Doctrine

I have the Word of God as my doctrine and I will avoid those who teach and preach otherwise.

Bible Doctrine

The Scriptures Inspired - The Bible teaches that Scripture is the inspired and only infallible and authoritative written Word of God.

Read 2 Timothy 3:10-17 from your Bible.

How much of the Bible is inspired of God? (verse 16)

_____

The One True God - The Bible teaches one God, eternally existent, in three persons; God the Father, God the Son, and God the Holy Ghost.

Read 1 John 5:6-13 from your Bible.

List the three names of the members of the Godhead as given in verse 7.

_____

The Deity Of The Lord Jesus Christ - The Bible teaches the deity of the Lord Jesus Christ. It declares: His virgin birth, His sinless life, His miracles, His substitutionary work on the cross, His bodily resurrection from the dead, His exaltation to the right hand of God.

Read John 20:24-29 from your Bible.

Who was the first disciple to recognize Jesus as God? (verse 28)

_____

The Fall of Man - The Bible teaches the fall of mankind and that the only means of being cleansed from sin is through repentance and faith in the precious blood of Christ.

Read Romans 3:21-26 from your Bible.

Is there anyone who has not sinned? (verse 23)

_____

The Salvation of Man - The Bible teaches that regeneration by the Holy Spirit is absolutely essential for personal salvation.

Read Titus 3:4-8 from your Bible.

List three blessings of God that are present in man's salvation. (verse 5)

_____

Bible Basics for Spirit-filled Believers

Ordinances Of The Church - The Bible teaches Water Baptism by immersion, and Holy Communion.

Read Matthew 28:16-20 from your Bible.

Jesus commanded believers to be baptized in what name? (verse 19)

_____

Read 1 Corinthians 11:23-26 from your Bible.

When we celebrate Holy Communion who are we remembering?

_____

The Baptism In The Holy Ghost - The Bible teaches the baptism in the Holy Spirit, which includes the empowerment to speak with tongues along with other spiritual gifts and fruit, is given to believers who ask.

Read Acts 1:4-8 from your Bible.

What does the Baptism in the Holy Spirit give the believer? (verse 8)

_____

Read Acts 2:1-4 from your Bible.

What did the disciples do when they were filled with the Holy Spirit?

_____

Read 1 Corinthians 12:1-11 from your Bible.

List the nine gifts of the Spirit. (verses 8-10)

_____

_____

Read Galatians 5:16-26 from your Bible.

List the nine fruit of the Spirit. (verses 22-23)

_____

_____

_____

Bible Doctrine

Sanctification - The Bible teaches the sanctifying power of the Holy Spirit by whose indulging the Christian is enabled to live a holy life.

Read 1 Thessalonians 5:23 from your Bible.

What are the three parts of the believer God wants to sanctify?

_____

The Church And Its Mission - The Bible teaches the ministry and mission of the Church for the spreading of the Gospel and the establishment of the Kingdom of God.

Read Ephesians 1:15-23 from your Bible.

What does Paul call the Church? (verse 23)

_____

The Ministry - The Bible teaches a God called and ordained ministry.

Read Ephesians 4:7-16 from your Bible.

List the different ministries Paul mentions. (verse 11)

_____

_____

Divine Healing - The Bible teaches the redemptive work of Christ on the cross provides healing of the human body in answer to believing prayer.

Read Matthew 8:16-17 from your Bible.

What two things did Christ bare for us on the cross? (verse 17)

_____

The Blessed Hope - The Bible teaches the rapture of the Church at Christ's coming.

Read 1 Thessalonians 4:13-18 from your Bible.

Why should this teaching be a comfort to believers?

_____

Bible Basics for Spirit-filled Believers

The Final Judgment - The Bible teaches the resurrection of the saved and the lost, one to everlasting life, the other to everlasting damnation.

Read Revelation 20:11-15 from your Bible.

Who are those who stand before God in this judgment? (verse 15)

_____

The New Heavens And The New Earth - The Bible teaches the new Heavens and the new Earth.

Read 2 Peter 3:10-13 from your Bible.

What is going to be the character of those who dwell in the new heavens and the new earth? (verse 13)

_____

Chapter 4 Assignments

❑ **Bible Reading**

Read chapters 4 - 21 in the book of John, and chapters 1 - 3 in the book of Acts.

❑ **Memory Verse**

Romans 16:17 Now I beseech you, brethren, mark them which cause divisions and offences contrary to the doctrine which ye have learned; and avoid them.

❑ **Speak The Word**

I have the Word of God as my doctrine and I will avoid those who teach and preach otherwise.

❑ **Prayer Time**

In your prayer time ask God to help you to learn sound doctrine from his Word. Ask for protection from those who would preach doctrines of devils. Also pray for your Pastor as he studies God's Word this week. Ask God to give him revelation of His Word so that he will be able to feed the congregation sound doctrine when the church comes together for worship.

Bible Doctrine

Journal/Notes

_____
_____
_____
_____
_____
_____
_____
_____
_____
_____
_____
_____
_____
_____
_____
_____
_____
_____
_____
_____
_____
_____
_____
_____
_____

Prayer

As a believer I abide in Christ, and as an obedient student of the Word, His words abide in me, therefore I ask what I will according to His Word and it is done unto me.

Prayer

Introduction

The Bible is the main way that God speaks to us. Prayer is our way of speaking to God. Prayer in its most basic form is simply "talking to God." Prayer is offering up of our desires for lawful and needful things that are promised by God, with the humble confidence that we will obtain them through Jesus Christ for God's glory and our good.

It is through prayer that we develop our relationship and enjoy fellowship with God. Without prayer, God seems to be very distant. With prayer God becomes our very best friend. This lesson will teach you how to have a fruitful and productive prayer life.

God's Promise To Hear And Answer Our Prayers

Read Jeremiah 33:1-3 from your Bible.

When we call unto God, what does He promise to show us? (verse 3)

_____

Three Reasons To Pray

1. Prayer is our way of having fellowship with God.

Read Luke 6:12-16 from your Bible.

What happens when we spend time with God in prayer, as in verse 12?

_____

2. Prayer blesses our inner man.

Read Psalms 16:1-11 from your Bible.

What two things are found in the presence of God? (verse 11)

_____

3. Prayer is the way we receive from God.

Read Matthew 7:7-12 from your Bible.

What three words in these verses are descriptive of prayer? (verse 7)

_____

Bible Basics for Spirit-filled Believers

Principles For Effective Prayer

1. Begin your prayer in an attitude of worship.

Read Psalms 100:1-5 from your Bible.

How are we to enter into the presence of God? (verse 4)

_____

2. Address your prayer to God the Father.

Read Matthew 6:5-13 from your Bible.

What two words does the Lord's prayer begin with? (verse 9)

_____

3. Pray in the name of Jesus.

Read John 16:16-33 from your Bible.

When we pray in Jesus name, what does Jesus do for us? (verse 26)

_____

4. Pray in line with God's will; His Word.

Read 1 John 5:14-17 from your Bible.

What happens when we pray according to God's will? (verse 14)

_____

5. Pray in faith and refuse all doubt.

Read James 1:2-8 from your Bible.

If we do not pray in faith what does James say happens? (verse 7)

_____

6. Allow the Holy Spirit to help you pray.

Read Romans 8:26-28 from your Bible.

When the Holy Spirit prays through us, what can we know? (verse 28)

_____

Prayer

7. Always end your prayer with praise.

Read Philippians 4:4-7 from your Bible.

What will our attitude be as we conclude our prayer? (verse 7)

How To Make Prayer A Part Of Your Daily Life

1. Set a time to pray.

Read Psalms 63:1-2 from your Bible.

Considering verse 1, what time is a good time for you to pray each day?

---

2. Designate a place for prayer.

Read Matthew 6:5-8 from your Bible.

What place is available to you where you can be alone with God?

---

3. Determine to pray for a specific amount of time each day.

Read Matthew 26:36-46 from your Bible.

What level of prayer time do you feel the Lord is calling you to?

---

4. Keep a prayer list, or a journal.

Read 1 Timothy 2:1-4 from your Bible.

Would a list or journal help you in fulfilling your prayer time?

---

5. Be faithful in your commitment to pray on a daily basis.

Read Galatians 6:6-10 from your Bible.

What promise are we given in verse 9 if we make prayer a daily habit?

Bible Basics for Spirit-filled Believers

The Practice Of Prayer

In this lesson you have learned much about what the Bible has to say about prayer. However, the most important part of this lesson is for you to experience prayer for yourself. Right now you should begin to pray. Use your own words and speak to God out of your heart. Do not worry or be concerned about how you sound to yourself or to anyone else. Remember God loves you just as you are and He is delighted to hear from you.

Chapter 5 Assignments

❑ **Bible Reading**

Read chapters 4 - 28 in the book of Acts.

❑ **Memory Verse**

John 15:7 If ye abide in me, and my words abide in you, ye shall ask what ye will, and it shall be done unto you.

❑ **Speak The Word**

As a believer I abide in Christ, and as a obedient student of the Word, His words abide in me, therefore I ask what I will according to His Word and it is done unto me.

❑ **Prayer Time**

Begin to set aside time each day to talk to God in prayer. Talk to Him just as you would your very best friend. Right now take the time to fulfill the instructions of section "How To Make Prayer A Part Of Your Daily Life." All new things take time and discipline. As you make this prayer commitment to God, you will begin to build an unshakable foundation for Christian growth, and maturity in Christ.

Prayer

Journal/Notes

Worship

I worship God in all of my ways, from the depth of my heart, in spirit and in truth.

Worship

Introduction

Worship is: those words, actions and attitudes which revere and honor the worthiness of God. Worship is an encounter with God. In this lesson we will learn to worship, as a true encounter with God.

Five Pre-requisites To Worship

1. Revelation - You must know God.

Read John 4:1-26 from your Bible.

Why is it important to know God in order to worship? (verse 22)

_____

2. Relationship - You must be in the family.

Read John 4:1-26 from your Bible.

What is your relationship to the name used of God in verse 23?

_____

3. Recognition - That you must worship in the spirit.

Read John 4:1-26 from your Bible.

Where must we recognize that our worship takes place? (verse 24)

_____

4. Reality - Worship must not be a outward form only.

Read Matthew 15:1-9 from your Bible.

What does Christ say is vain worship? (verse 8)

_____

5. Righteous - We cannot worship if we are living a sinful lifestyle.

Read Isaiah 1:1-20 from your Bible.

Why did God turn away from His people? (verse 4)

_____

Bible Basics for Spirit-filled Believers

Nine Elements Of New Testament Worship

1. Prayer.

Read Acts 1:12-14 from your Bible.

Do you think prayer played a part in keeping the Church in one accord?

_____

2. Singing.

Read Ephesians 5:15-21 from your Bible.

What three kinds of songs are to be sung in worship? (verse 19)

_____

3. Praise.

Read Hebrews 13:7-17 from your Bible.

What two things is praise compared to? (verse 15)

_____

4. Confession of sin.

Read Matthew 6:9-13 from your Bible.

What two ways does forgiveness extend in the Lord's Prayer? (verse 12)

_____

5. Scripture reading and study.

Read 2 Timothy 2:15 from your Bible.

How do you think that the study of the Word will help you to worship?

_____

6. Preaching of the Word.

Read 2 Timothy 4:1-5 from your Bible.

Worship

List three ways the Word is preached. (verse 2)

_____

7. Holy Communion and Baptism in water.

Read Acts 2:40-47 from your Bible.

Do you feel that participating in these ordinances is worship? Why?

_____

8. Tithes and Offerings.

Read Malachi 3:8-12 from your Bible.

As we worship by our giving, what does God do for us? (verse 11)

_____

9. Signs and wonders.

Read 1 Corinthians 12:1-11 from your Bible.

How do signs and wonders affect our worship?

_____

A Biblical Example Of Powerful Worship

Read Isaiah 6:1-8 from your Bible

Match the subjects with the correct verses.

Worship is taking place   Verse _____

Isaiah confesses his sin.   Verse _____

Isaiah receives an anointing from the altar.   Verse _____

Isaiah is released from the bondage of his sin.   Verse _____

Isaiah dedicates himself to God's service.   Verse _____

Bible Basics for Spirit-filled Believers

List the different expressions of worship that are mentioned in the following Psalms:

Psalms 5:11 _____

Psalms 47:1 _____

Psalms 63:4 _____

Psalms 149:1 _____

Psalms 149:3 _____

Psalms 150:3-5 _____

A Note About Worship

Worship may be expressed in many different ways. However, all Biblical worship will always glorify God, and be decent and in order. *1 Corinthians 14:40*

Chapter 6 Assignments

❑ **Bible Reading**

Read chapters 1 - 16 in the book of Romans, and chapters 1 - 6 in the book of 1 Corinthians.

❑ **Memory Verse**

John 4:24 God is a Spirit: and they that worship him must worship him in spirit and in truth.

❑ **Speak The Word**

I worship God in all of my ways, from the depth of my heart, in spirit and in truth.

❑ **Prayer Time**

In prayer of course we always worship God, but this week in your prayer time, try spending a greater amount of time in worship toward God. Think about your relationships with others. Do you enjoy people always asking of you, or sometimes, is it nice just to know that they love you and enjoy being with you. Let us never fail to show God our love and joy of just being in His presence.

Worship

Journal/Notes

Tithing

I pay tithes of all of my income, therefore the house of the Lord is full and the windows of heaven are open to me. God is pouring out abundant blessings into my life.

Tithing

Introduction

The Bible tells us in *Psalms 24:1 The earth is the Lord's*. As God's greatest creation, we are lent the earth during our lifetime. Because of this, we will be held accountable to God for our use of His possessions. The money God allows us to have is included in this accountability. Many Christians have no problem when it comes to God's money, others however, seem to find money as a major testing ground of their faith. The problem arises because of not knowing the Bible where giving is concerned or because of not fully surrendering possessions to the Lordship of Christ.In this lesson we will study the Bible doctrine of tithing. We will learn that in fact, tithing is God's plan of blessing both for our Church and our own personal lives.

What Is The Tithe

1. The tithe is our way of honoring God.

Read Proverbs 3:9-10 from your Bible.

What part of our increase are we to honor God with?

_____

2. The tithe belongs to God.

Read Leviticus 27:30 from your Bible.

What two kinds of tithe does this verse mention?

_____

What is the tithe called?

_____

When Did Tithing Begin

1. Abraham paid tithes to God.

Read Genesis 14:8-24 from your Bible.

Of what part of Abraham's blessings did he pay tithes? (verse 20)

_____

Bible Basics for Spirit-filled Believers

2. Jacob paid tithes to God.

Read Genesis 28:10-22 from your Bible.

Do you think that tithing is a partnership relationship with God? Why?

_____

3. The children of Abraham and Jacob were blessed through tithing.

Read Genesis 26:1-14 from your Bible.

What was in the land that brought everyone poverty? (verse 1)

_____

In the troubled time, did God bless Isaac? With how much? (verse 12)

_____

What Is The Purpose Of Tithing

1. Tithing is a means of worship.

Read Deuteronomy 26:1-19 from your Bible.

In verses 10 and 11 what are we told to do when we bring our tithes?

_____

2. Tithing is a means of obeying the Words of Jesus.

Read Matthew 23:23 from your Bible.

What did Jesus say concerning paying tithes?

_____

3. Tithing provides financial support for the local church.

Read Malachi 3:8-12 from your Bible.

Would your church survive if everyone just gave offerings each week?

_____

Tithing

God Warns Against Withholding The Tithe

Read Malachi 3:8-12 from your Bible.

What does God call the failure to pay tithes? (verse 8)

_____

Blessings Are Directly Related To Our Tithing & Giving

1. We determine the amount of our increase from God.

Read 2 Corinthians 9:6-15 from your Bible.

How does a person reap who gives sparingly and bountifully? (verse 6)

_____

2. Our tithing sets up an account with God.

Read Philippians 4:10-20 from your Bible.

Because of the Philippians support of Paul's ministry, who did Paul say would share the credit for the work of his ministry? (verse 17)

_____

Who then is promised to have all their needs supplied? (Cp. 14 & 19)

_____

God's Promises To The Tither

1. Divine protection.

Read Malachi 3:8-12 from your Bible.

Who will be rebuked when we give God His tithes? (verse 11)

_____

2. Material blessings.

Read Proverbs 3:9-10 from your Bible.

Bible Basics for Spirit-filled Believers

What does God say He will do for the person who gives their first fruits?

_____

Read Luke 6:38 from your Bible.

How did Jesus say God measures our blessings back to us?

_____

3. Eternal rewards.

Read Matthew 6:19-21 from your Bible.

If a person really treasures God, will he have a problem in giving?

_____

Chapter 7 Assignments

❏ **Bible Reading**

Read chapters 7 - 16 in the book of 1 Corinthians, and chapters 1 - 13 in the book of 2 Corinthians.

❏ **Memory Verse**

Malachi 3:10 Bring ye all the tithes into the storehouse, that there may be meat in mine house, and prove me now herewith, saith the Lord of hosts, if I will not open you the windows of heaven, and pour you out a blessing, that there shall not be room enough to receive it.

❏ **Speak The Word**

I pay tithes of all of my income, therefore the house of the Lord is full and the windows of heaven are open to me. God is pouring out abundant blessings into my life.

❏ **Prayer Time**

As you pray, begin to claim the blessings of the tither which you have studied in this lesson. Pray for the needs of your Church, your family, and yourself. Claim the promise of Malachi 3:10-11 that the devourer is rebuked out of your life.

Tithing

Journal/Notes

_____

_____

_____

_____

_____

_____

_____

_____

_____

_____

_____

_____

_____

_____

_____

_____

_____

_____

_____

_____

_____

_____

Witnessing

I am empowered by the
Holy Spirit to be a
witness of the Lord. I
am a witness; all the
time, in every place, to
everyone.

Witnessing

Introduction

Webster says that a witness is "one who furnishes evidence or proof; one who has seen or has knowledge of an incident; or one who attests to another person." From a Biblical understanding, a witness is one who first has received the gospel himself, and then proclaims that truth to others. Witnessing takes places in both words and actions. Witnessing is more than an activity that we do, it is a way of life.

In this chapter we will learn why we should witness, how to be an effective witness and how to tear down barriers in our lives that keep us from telling the world about what Christ has done in our lives and what he wants to do for all who will believe.

Why Believers Should Be Witnesses

1. Witnessing is a command of the Lord Jesus.

Read Mark 16:14-18 from your Bible.

What happens when people respond to our witness? (verse 16)

_____

2. Witnessing the Gospel is the only means of salvation.

Read Romans 10:13-17 from your Bible.

Before a person can call upon God, what is needed? (verse 14)

_____

3. The believer is held accountable for witnessing.

Read Ezekiel 3:17-27 from your Bible.

What does God require at our hands if we fail to witness? (verse 18)

_____

4. Without receiving the witness of Christ no one can be saved.

Read 1 Corinthians 1:18-25 from your Bible.

What is necessary in order for a person to be saved? (verse 21)

_____

Bible Basics for Spirit-filled Believers

How To Be An Effective Witness

1. Allow the love of God to motivate you to witness.

Read Galatians 5:14 from your Bible.

If we love our neighbor, what is the greatest thing we could do for him?

_____

2. Witness through the life that you live.

Read Matthew 5:13-16 from your Bible.

What does Jesus say that men should see in us? (verse 16)

_____

3. Witness by the power of the Word.

Read 1 Peter 1:22-25 from your Bible.

What causes the new birth to take place in people's lives? (verse 23)

_____

Philip's Example In Witnessing

Read Acts 8:26-40 from your Bible.

Locate the verses which match these thoughts.

Being led by the Holy Spirit.   Verse _____

Being obedient to the Lord's command.   Verse _____

Being sensitive to the Ethiopian's need.   Verse _____

Having a knowledge of the Word of God.   Verse _____

Leading in a decision for Christ.   Verse _____

Having boldness to act.   Verse _____

Think about these qualities and how they would be useful in helping you to witness to others about the love of Christ.

Witnessing

Barriers To Witnessing And Overcoming Them

1. Lethargy or having no desire to witness.

Read Mark 9:43-48 from your Bible.

Is there anything more important than helping someone to miss hell?

---

2. The fear of man.

Read Proverbs 29:25 from your Bible.

How can you feel safe in your witnessing?

---

3. Saying I will witness another day.

Read John 4:27-38 from your Bible.

Is the harvest ready to be reaped yet? (verse 35)

---

4. I don't know how to speak to people about Christ.

Read 1 Peter 3:15 from your Bible.

What should our response be when someone ask us about Christ?

---

5. I am ashamed to speak for Christ.

Read 2 Timothy 1:8-12 from your Bible.

According to verse 8 what is available to us to overcome being ashamed?

Read Mark 8:34-38 from your Bible.

Think about the consequences of being ashamed of Christ in this world.

Bible Basics for Spirit-filled Believers

The Romans Road To Salvation - A Great Witnessing Tool

Look up and read each of the Scriptures in the Romans Road to Salvation below. You should memorize them or write them in the flyleaf of your Bible, so that you will always be ready to share this simple plan of salvation, with those who are lost.

1.All have sinned.
Read Romans 3:23 from your Bible.

2. Sin has a penalty.
Read Romans 6:23a from your Bible.

3. God loves the sinner and has already paid the sin penalty.
Read Romans 5:8 from your Bible.

4. Salvation is a free gift.
Read Romans 6:23b from your Bible.

5. Salvation is received by belief and confession on Jesus Christ.
Read Romans 10:9-10 from your Bible.

Chapter 8 Assignments

❏ **Bible Reading**

Read chapters 1 - 6 in the book of Galatians; 1 - 6 in the book of Ephesians; 1 - 4 in the book of Philippians; 1 - 4 in the book of Colossians; and 1 - 2 in the book of 1 Thessalonians.

❏ **Memory Verse**

Acts 1:8 But ye shall receive power, after that the Holy Ghost is come upon you: and ye shall be witnesses unto me both in Jerusalem, and in all Judaea, and in Samaria, and unto the uttermost part of the earth.

❏ **Speak The Word**

I am empowered by the Holy Spirit to be a witness of the Lord. I am a witness; all the time, in every place, to everyone.

❏ **Prayer Time**

Make a list of those you would like to see receive Jesus as saviour. You can list members of your family; those at your work place; people where you shop; unsaved people who attend your church and any others the Holy Spirit brings to your mind. Pray for them each day.

Witnessing

Journal/Notes

_____

_____

_____

_____

_____

_____

_____

_____

_____

_____

_____

_____

_____

_____

_____

_____

_____

_____

_____

_____

_____

_____

_____

_____

Living by Faith

As God's Word fills my heart, and I make it the confession of my mouth, God will cause me to have whatsoever I say.

Living By Faith

Introduction

Faith is an inner knowing, which convinces the spirit of man of the things not seen. It does not depend on the aid of the five senses and leaves no options of thought, concern, or another course of action, which would be contrary to the Word of God, which produces the faith.

In this chapter we will study the power of living a life of faith.

The Bible Definition Of Faith

1. Faith is the reality of things not seen.

Read Hebrews 11:1-3 from your Bible.

Write down the meaning of faith in your own words. (verse 1)

_____

2. Faith is calling those things which be not as though they were.

Read Romans 4:13-25 from your Bible.

May we as believers speak as God speaks? (verse 17)

_____

Faith Is An Unfailing Law Of God

1. Faith is a law (principle or rule) of God.

Read Romans 3:21-31 from your Bible.

Does a believer live by the law of works, or the law of faith? (verse 27)

_____

2. The law of faith in action and stated.

Read Matthew 9:27-31 from your Bible.

Write down the "law of faith;" the last half of verse 29.

_____

_____

Bible Basics for Spirit-filled Believers

The Importance Of Living By Faith.

1. Faith is the key to all the blessings of God.

Read Mark 9:14-29 from your Bible.

What becomes possible to the person who will believe? (verse 23)

_____

2. The greatest weapon of warfare the believer has is faith?

Read Ephesians 6:10-20 from your Bible.

What will the shield of faith do in our lives? (verse 16)

_____

3. It is only through living by faith that we can please God.

Read Hebrews 11:4-7 from your Bible.

What two things must we believe when we live by faith? (verse 6)

_____

How To Increase Your Faith.

1. Realize faith is not something you get, it is something you have.

Read Romans 12:1-3 from your Bible.

Would it be truthful to say; "I just don't have any faith?" (verse 3)

_____

2. Faith is increased by hearing the Word of God.

Read Romans 10:14-17 from your Bible.

According to verse 17, how does faith come?

_____

Living By Faith

Jesus The Master Teacher Of Faith And Its Operation

Read Mark 11:20-24 from your Bible.

Match the subjects with the correct verses.

Have faith in God.	Verse _____
Anyone may use faith.	Verse _____
All doubt must be removed.	Verse _____
You must believe in what you say.	Verse _____
Believing starts at the time of prayer.	Verse _____
You shall receive.	Verse _____

The Operation Of Faith In The Life Of The Believer

1. Read the Word.

Read Romans 10:14-17 from your Bible.

Does faith come by hearing just any religious writing? (verse 17)

_____

2. Meditate (mutter, speak and confess) the Word.

Read Joshua 1:1-9 from your Bible.

What happens when we meditate the Word? (verse 8)

_____

3. Pray the Word.

Read Mark 11:20-24 from your Bible.

What must we believe when we pray? (verse 24)

_____

4. Act on the Word.

Read James 1:21-27 from your Bible.

What happens when we are hearers only? (verse 22) A doer? (verse 25)

_____

Bible Basics for Spirit-filled Believers

Blessings Come Through Faith

Look up and read each of the Scriptures following the blessings below.

1. Salvation is received through faith. *Luke 7:36-50; Acts 8:26-40*

2. The Holy Spirit is received through faith. *Galatians 3:1-9; 3:10-14*

3. Access to God's presence is through faith. *Romans 3:21-31; 5:1-5*

4. Prayer is answered through faith. *Matthew 21:20-22; James 1:2-8*

5. Prosperity is received through faith. *1 Kings 17:8-16; Luke 6:37-38*

6. Healing is received through faith. *Mark 5:21-43; James 5:13-18*

7. All victory is received through faith. *1 John 5:1-5; Hebrews 11:1-40*

Chapter 9 Assignments

❏ **Bible Reading**

Read chapters 3 - 5 in the book of 1 Thessalonians; chapters 1 - 3 in the book of 2 Thessalonians chapters 1 - 6 in 1 Timothy; chapters 1 - 4 in 2 Timothy; chapters 1 - 3 in the book of Titus; and the book of Philemon.

❏ **Memory Verse**

Mark 11:23 For verily I say unto you, That whosoever shall say unto this mountain, Be thou removed, and be thou cast into the sea; and shall not doubt in his heart, but shall believe that those things which he saith shall come to pass; he shall have whatsoever he saith.

24 Therefore I say unto you, What things soever ye desire, when ye pray, believe that ye receive them, and ye shall have them.

❏ **Speak The Word**

As God's Word fills my heart, and I make it the confession of my mouth, God will cause me to have whatsoever I say.

❏ **Prayer Time**

Pray the Word, believe you receive, and you shall have it.

Living By Faith

Journal/Notes

The Baptism in the Holy Spirit

Jesus is my baptizer, He does all things well. As I submit to Him, I am filled, and am continually being refilled with the Spirit.

The Baptism in the Holy Spirit

Introduction

The baptism in the Spirit is one of the most misunderstood experiences of the Christian world. However, this experience is one of the greatest blessings a Christian can receive. In this chapter we will study the truth of the Bible concerning this wonderful experience.

There Is A Baptism In The Holy Spirit

1. All four Gospels teach that Jesus would baptize with the Spirit.

Read Mat. 3:11; Mk. 1:8; Lk.3:16; & Jn.1:33 from your Bible.

If the Bible mentions something one time is it important? Four times?

_____

Jesus And The Baptism In The Holy Spirit

1. Jesus was baptized with the Spirit.

Read Matthew 3:13-17 from your Bible.

What happened when Jesus was baptized with the Spirit? (verse 16)

_____

2. Jesus said his disciples would also be baptized with the Spirit.

Read Matthew 20:22-23 from your Bible.

Are disciples able to receive spiritual blessings like Jesus receives?

_____

3. Jesus was anointed with the Holy Ghost.

Read Acts 10:38 from your Bible.

What was the effect of Jesus being anointed with the Holy Spirit?

_____

Do you believe the Spirit could anoint you to do the works of Jesus?

_____

Bible Basics for Spirit-filled Believers

The Believer And The Baptism In The Holy Spirit

1. Believers receive the Holy Spirit in a measure at the New Birth.

Read Romans 8:8-17 from your Bible.

If a person belongs to God, then does the Spirit dwell in him? (verse 9)

_____

2. The baptism in the Holy Spirit is not the same as the New Birth.

Read Acts 19:1-7 from your Bible.

According to verse 2 how many spiritual experiences are mentioned?

_____

3. Jesus commanded believers to be baptized in the Holy Spirit.

Read Acts 1:4-8 from your Bible.

If Jesus commands his disciples, what should the response be?

_____

4. The first outpouring of the Holy Spirit upon believers.

Read Acts 2:1-4 from your Bible.

What were the two signs of the Holy Spirit coming into the earth?

_____

What was the sign of the Holy Spirit coming into the believers?

_____

What The Baptism In The Holy Spirit Is

Read Luke 24:49; Acts 1:8; and John 14:12 from your Bible.

Match the subjects with the correct Scripture passages.
Being endued with power.   Scripture _____
The power to witness.   Scripture _____
Doing the works of Christ.   Scripture _____

The Baptism in the Holy Spirit

Proofs The Baptism In The Holy Spirit Is For You

1. The Spirit is a gift promised to all believers God has called.

Read Acts 2:38-39 from your Bible.

Have you been called to salvation? Then may you have the promise?

_____

2. Peter promised the outpouring of the Spirit in our day.

Read Acts 2:17-18 from your Bible.

Who was the Holy Spirit promised to be poured out upon?

_____

3. Jesus redeemed us from our sins and to empower us.

Read Galatians 3:10-14 from your Bible.

What promise are we to receive by faith? (verse 14)

_____

How To Receive The Baptism In The Holy Spirit

1. You must be born again.

Read Acts 2:38 from your Bible.

What comes before receiving the gift of the Holy Spirit?

_____

2. Truly make Jesus Lord of your life and obey Him in all things.

Read Acts 5:22-32 from your Bible.

Who does God give the Holy Spirit to? (verse 32)

_____

Bible Basics for Spirit-filled Believers

3. Have a genuine hunger and thirst.

Read Matthew 5:1-12 from your Bible.

What promise is given for those who hunger and thirst? (verse 6)

_____

4. Ask God to fill you with the Holy Spirit.

Read Luke 11:9-13 from your Bible.

Who does God give the Holy Spirit to? (verse 13)

_____

5. Begin to praise God for the Spirit as you receive Him by faith.

Read Acts 1:14; 2:1-4; and 2:11 from your Bible.

Chapter 10 Assignments

❑ **Bible Reading**

Read chapters 1 -13 in the book of Hebrews; chapters 1 - 5 in the book of James; and chapters 1 - 3 in the book of 1 Peter.

❑ **Memory Verse**

Matthew 3:11 I indeed baptize you with water unto repentance: but he that cometh after me is mightier than I, whose shoes I am not worthy to bear: he shall baptize you with the Holy Ghost, and with fire:

❑ **Speak The Word**

Jesus is my baptizer. He does all things well. As I submit to Him, I am filled, and am continually being refilled with the Spirit.

❑ **Prayer Time**

As you pray, if you are not filled with the Spirit, ask Jesus to fill you. If you are filled with the Spirit, allow the Holy Spirit to empower your prayer life through the use of Spiritual gifts. Always allow time for the leading of the Spirit as you pray. Yield to Him daily and be sensitive to His leading in your life.

The Baptism in the Holy Spirit

Journal/Notes

_____

_____

_____

_____

_____

_____

_____

_____

_____

_____

_____

_____

_____

_____

_____

_____

_____

_____

_____

_____

_____

_____

_____

_____

_____

_____

Divine Healing

I bless the Lord and remember all his benefits. He forgives all my sins and heals all my diseases.

Divine Healing

Introduction

Healing can be looked at as three types. 1) Natural healing which takes place as the God given ability of the body heals itself. A cut for example will stop the blood flow by coagulation and then scab over, giving time for repair and the growth of new skin. 2) Healing of the body aided by medical science, which happens when men use knowledge and medicines that are given by God, to heal the body. 3) Divine healing of the body without the aid of the body or man. This kind of healing is by "God alone." This healing is Divine. It is Divine healing.

It Is God's Will To Heal The Sick

1. The Apostle John states healing is God's will.

Read 3 John 1:1-4 from your Bible.

List the three areas of prosperity God desires for His children. (verse 2)

_____

2. Jesus healed all who asked Him during His earthly ministry.

Read Luke 6:17-19 from your Bible.

Of all the multitude that wanted to touch Him how many were healed?

_____

Healing Is Part Of The Atonement Of Christ

1. Isaiah said that the atonement covered both sins and sickness.

Read Isaiah 53:1-6 from your Bible.

Write the last portion of verse 5.

_____

2. Matthew in the New Testament confirms the words of Isaiah.

Read Matthew 8:14-17 from your Bible.

What did Matthew record that the prophet Isaiah said? (verse 17)

_____

_____

Bible Basics for Spirit-filled Believers

Reasons Healing Has Not Passed Away

1. Jesus is a healer and He has never changed.

Read Acts 10:38 and Hebrews 13:8 from your Bible.

What was the ministry of Jesus? Has that ministry changed?

_____

2. Disciples prayed for the sick and true disciples never change.

Read Luke 10:1-12 and John 8:31 from your Bible.

For disciples to continue in the Word of Jesus, what must that include?

_____

Seven Hindrances To Receiving Healing

1. A lack of sincere desire to be healed.

Read James 5:13-18 from your Bible.

What kind of prayer avails much? (verse 16)

_____

2. Continued physical abuse of the body.

Read Galatians 6:6-8 from your Bible.

Do you think that the way a man treats his body can hinder healing?

_____

3. A failure to set a certain time for healing.

Read Mark 5:25-34 from your Bible.

At what time did the woman say she would be healed? (verse 28)

_____

_____

Divine Healing

4. A prayer that does not recognize Satan's part in sickness.

Read Matthew 9:32-33 from your Bible.

When did the man receive his healing? (verse 33)

_____

5. Ignorance concerning the will of God to heal.

Read Matthew 8:1-4 from your Bible.

Is an "if it be thou will" prayer needed where the will of God is known?

_____

6. A lack of faith for healing.

Read Mark 6:1-6 from your Bible.

Why could not even Jesus heal in his own country? (verse 6)

_____

7. Un-confessed sin in a person's life.

Read Psalms 66:18 from your Bible.

Will God hear us if we allow sin to reign in our hearts? _____

Steps To Take To Receive Healing

1. Know that the age of miracles has not passed away.

Read Exodus 15:26 from your Bible.

Is God an "I was" or "I use to" or "I can't anymore" or an "I am?"

_____

2. Know it is Satan who wants you sick and God who wants you well.

Read John 10:7-21 from your Bible.

What three things does Satan want to do? (verse 10)

_____

Bible Basics for Spirit-filled Believers

3. Ask God to heal you.

Read James 4:1-2 from your Bible.

Why do we sometimes fail to receive from God? (verse 2)

_____

4. Believe when prayer is offered that you are healed.

Read Mark 11:22-24 from your Bible.

At what time do you begin to believe for healing? (verse 24)

_____

5. Begin to praise God in faith for your healing.

Read Romans 4:13-21 from your Bible.

Because Abraham was strong in faith, what did he do? (verse 20)

Chapter 11 Assignments

❑ **Bible Reading**

Read chapters 4 -5 in the book of 1 Peter; 1 - 3 in the book of 2 Peter; 1 - 5 in the book of 1 John; the book of 2 John; the book of 3 John; and the book of Jude.

❑ **Memory Verse**

Psalms 103:2 Bless the LORD, O my soul, and forget not all his benefits: 3 Who forgiveth all thine iniquities; who healeth all thy diseases;

❑ **Speak The Word**

I bless the Lord and remember all his benefits. He forgives all my sins and heals all my diseases.

❑ **Prayer Time**

In prayer, thank God for healing your body. If you have physical needs ask Him to heal you. When you pray believe that it is done and receive it by faith. Have compassion for and pray for the healing of others as well.

Divine Healing

Journal/Notes

_____
_____
_____
_____
_____
_____
_____
_____
_____
_____
_____
_____
_____
_____
_____
_____
_____
_____
_____
_____
_____
_____
_____
_____

The Church

Christ has built His church. His church will not fail. Because I am born again, I am in His church. Being in His church all of hell cannot prevail against me.

The Church

Introduction

The word church means "called out." The church is therefore a called out body of believers from all people, who have been born again. It includes both those born again on earth and those who are now in heaven.

In this chapter we will study the Biblical meaning of the church and its wonderful operation in the earth.

Jesus And The Church

1. Jesus is the creator and founder of the church.

Read Matthew 16:13-20 from your Bible.

Will Satan be able to defeat the Lord's church? (verse 18)

_____

2. Jesus is the head of the church.

Read Ephesians 5:22-33 from your Bible.

To what does Paul compare the church to?

_____

3. Jesus' church is called the Body of Christ.

Read Ephesians 1:15-23 from your Bible.

In verse 22 what does it mean to have all things under the churches' feet?

_____

The Church Has Believers Who Serve In Ministry Offices

1. The ministry offices are God's gifts for the perfecting of the saints.

Read Ephesians 4:7-16 from your Bible.

List the ministry offices as given in verse 11.

_____

_____

Bible Basics for Spirit-filled Believers

Becoming An Active Participate Of The Church

1. The believer is to attend church regularly.

Read Hebrews 10:19-25 from your Bible.

What is the value of attending church on a regular basis?

_____

2. The believer is to support the church with tithes and offerings.

Read Malachi 3:8-12 from your Bible.

What two things happen when we support the church? (verse 10)

_____

3. The believer is to become a part of his new family.

Read Matthew 12:46-50 from your Bible.

Who is also a part of the family of the believer? (verse 50)

_____

4. The believer is to become involved in the ministry of the church.

Read Matthew 9:35-38 from your Bible.

What three things did Jesus do in ministering to the people? (verse 35)

_____

Can the church do more ministry if we all become involved? (verse 38)

_____

5. The believer is to submit himself to the leadership of the church.

Read Hebrews 13:7-17 from your Bible.

Is the leadership accountable to God? For who? Is this good for you?

_____

_____

The Church

How The Church Will Help You

1. The church will help you mature through the power of the Word.

Read 2 Timothy 3:10-17 from your Bible.

List three different times that the Word is heard at church services.

_____

2. The church will help you through the power of prayer.

Read Acts 12:5-19 from your Bible.

Who was doing the praying when Peter was in need? (verse 5)

_____

3. The church will help you in the worship of God.

Read Hebrews 13:15-16 from your Bible.

Is it easier to worship God in a atmosphere of praise such as the church?

_____

4. The church will help you by the fellowship of other Christians.

Read Philippians 1:1-11 from your Bible.

What was Paul thankful for in the Philippian church? (verse 5)

_____

5. The church will help you by providing you with Pastoral care.

Read Jeremiah 3:15 from your Bible.

What does Jeremiah say that Pastors do for God's children?

_____

Write down other ways that Pastors minister to believers.

_____

Bible Basics for Spirit-filled Believers

The Church Is God's Family For You

Read Psalms 68:6 from your Bible.

If we are obedient, will we dwell in a dry land or a family; the church?

The Church Is God's Earthly Home For His Children

The church is a called out group of believers, who have come together to do God's work of ministry in the earth. It participates in evangelism, discipleship, ministry, worship, fellowship and many other numerous blessings on behalf of Christ, to believers, and to the world.

The church consist of men and women just like yourself who are very human and fallible. There is no perfect church. But, there are many churches where people do their best to live Christ-like in all of their ways. If you have not fully given yourself in ministry to Christ by the way of His church, then make a decision to do so today.

Chapter 12 Assignments

❏ **Bible Reading**

Read chapters 1 - 22 in the book of Revelation.

❏ **Memory Verse**

Matthew 16:18 And I say also unto thee, That thou art Peter, and upon this rock I will build my church: and the gates of hell shall not prevail against it.

❏ **Speak The Word**

Christ has built His church. His church will not fail. Because I am born again, I am in His church. Being in His church all of hell cannot prevail against me.

❏ **Prayer Time**

Pray for your Church this week. Pray for the Pastor, elders, deacons, teachers, ministers, leadership, members, attendants, and all those who work to make it successful. Pray for the financial needs, and ministry outreaches. Pray for people to be saved, filled with the Spirit, healed, and blessed through the church ministry. Pray for unity and love. Ask God to show you how you can be a greater blessing to your church.

The Church

Journal/Notes

Ministry Helps

Complete this **Order Form** and process as follows:

Fax orders: (864) 682-5428
E-mail orders: orders@ministryhelps.com
On-line orders: http://www.ministryhelps.com
Telephone orders: (864) 682-5425. Have your credit card ready.
Postal orders: Ministry Helps, 746 Vern-Cora Road,
Laurens, South Carolina 29360

Quantity	Item	Cost	Total
	Bible Basics for Spirit-filled Believers	6.95	
	Tithe and Offering Scriptures - Red	19.95	
	Tithe and Offering Scriptures #2 - Blue	19.95	
	Tithe and Offering Scriptures #3 - Green	19.95	
	Tithe and Offering Scriptures #4 - Brown (Available Fall of 2002)	19.95	
	Sub Total		
	South Carolina residents add 5% sales tax		
	Shippng 10% of total - ($3.95 minimum)		
	Total		

Name:_____

Address:_____

City: _____ State: _____ Zip: _____

Credit card number: _____

Name on card: _____ Exp.Date: ____/____

Prices are subject to change as printing cost warrant.
Books are available at a considerable discount when purchased in quantity. Write for details.
100% satisfaction guaranteed or your money will be cheerfully refunded!

Progress Schedule

STUDY GUIDE CHAPTER 1 - The New Birth

Read and complete pages 6 - 11 in the Study Guide ❑

Bible Reading

Matthew	chapters 1- 3	❑
	chapters 4 - 6	❑
	chapters 7 - 9	❑
	chapters 10 - 12	❑
	chapters 13 - 15	❑
	chapters 16 - 18	❑
	chapters 19 - 21	❑

Scripture Memorization   Romans 10:9-10 ❑

STUDY GUIDE CHAPTER 2 - Discipleship

Read and complete pages 12 - 17 in the Study Guide ❑

Bible Reading

Matthew	chapters 22 - 24	❑
	chapters 25 - 28	❑
Mark	chapters 1 - 3	❑
	chapters 4 - 6	❑
	chapters 7 - 9	❑
	chapters 10 - 12	❑
	chapters 13 - 16	❑

Scripture Memorization   John 8:31 ❑

STUDY GUIDE CHAPTER 3 - The Bible

Read and complete pages 18 - 23 in the Study Guide ❑

Bible Reading

Luke	chapters 1 - 4	❑
	chapters 5 - 8	❑
	chapters 9 - 12	❑
	chapters 13 - 16	❑
	chapters 17 - 20	❑
	chapters 21 - 24	❑
John	chapters 1 - 3	❑

Scripture Memorization   2 Tim. 3:16-17 ❑

Progress Schedule

STUDY GUIDE CHAPTER 4 - Bible Doctrine

Read and complete pages 24 - 29 in the Study Guide ❏

Bible Reading

John	chapters 4 - 6	❏
	chapters 7 - 9	❏
	chapters 10 - 12	❏
	chapters 13 - 15	❏
	chapters 16 - 18	❏
	chapters 19 - 21	❏
Acts	chapters 1 - 3	❏

Scripture Memorization   Romans 16:17   ❏

STUDY GUIDE CHAPTER 5 - Prayer

Read and complete pages 30 - 35 in the Study Guide ❏

Bible Reading

Acts	chapters 4 - 7	❏
	chapters 8 - 10	❏
	chapters 11 - 14	❏
	chapters 15 - 17	❏
	chapters 18 - 21	❏
	chapters 22 - 24	❏
	chapters 25 - 28	❏

Scripture Memorization   John 15:7   ❏

STUDY GUIDE CHAPTER 6 - Worship

Read and complete pages 36 - 41 in the Study Guide ❏

Bible Reading

Romans	chapters 1 - 3	❏
	chapters 4 - 6	❏
	chapters 7 - 9	❏
	chapters 10 - 12	❏
	chapters 13 - 16	❏
1 Corinthians	chapters 1 - 3	❏
	chapters 4 - 6	❏

Scripture Memorization   John 4:24   ❏

Progress Schedule

STUDY GUIDE CHAPTER 7 - Tithing

Read and complete pages 42 - 47 in the Study Guide ❑

Bible Reading

1 Corinthians	chapters 7 - 9	❑
	chapters 10 - 12	❑
	chapters 13 - 16	❑
2 Corinthians	chapters 1 - 3	❑
	chapters 4 - 6	❑
	chapters 7 - 9	❑
	chapters 10 - 13	❑

Scripture Memorization   Malachi 3:10 ❑

STUDY GUIDE CHAPTER 8 - Witnessing

Read and complete pages 48 - 53 in the Study Guide ❑

Bible Reading

Galatians	chapters 1 - 3	❑
	chapters 4 - 6	❑
Ephesians	chapters 1 - 3	❑
	chapters 4 - 6	❑
Philippians	chapters 1 - 4	❑
Colossians	chapters 1 - 4	❑
1 Thessalonians	chapters 1 - 2	❑

Scripture Memorization   Acts 1:8 ❑

STUDY GUIDE CHAPTER 9 - Living by Faith

Read and complete pages 54 - 59 in the Study Guide ❑

Bible Reading

1 Thessalonians	chapters 3 - 5	❑
2 Thessalonians	chapters 1 - 3	❑
1 Timothy	chapters 1 - 3	❑
	chapters 4 - 6	❑
2 Timothy	chapters 1 - 4	❑
Titus	chapters 1 - 3	❑
Philemon	chapter 1	❑

Scripture Memorization   Mark 11:23-24 ❑

Progress Schedule

STUDY GUIDE CHAPTER 10 - The Baptism in the Holy Spirit

Read and complete pages 60 - 65 in the Study Guide ❏

Bible Reading

Hebrews	chapters 1 - 3	❏
	chapters 4 - 6	❏
	chapters 7 - 9	❏
	chapters 10 - 13	❏
James	chapters 1 - 3	❏
	chapters 4 - 5	❏
1 Peter	chapters 1 - 3	❏

Scripture Memorization   Matthew 3:11 ❏

STUDY GUIDE CHAPTER 11 - Divine Healing

Read and complete pages 66 - 71 in the Study Guide ❏

Bible Reading

1 Peter	chapters 4 - 5	❏
2 Peter	chapters 1 - 3	❏
1 John	chapters 1 - 3	❏
	chapters 4 - 5	❏
2 John	chapter 1	❏
3 John	chapter 1	❏
Jude	chapter 1	❏

Scripture Memorization   Psalms 103:2 - 3 ❏

STUDY GUIDE CHAPTER 12 - The Church

Read and complete pages 72 - 77 in the Study Guide ❏

Bible Reading

Revelation	chapters 1 - 3	❏
	chapters 4 - 6	❏
	chapters 7 - 9	❏
	chapters 10 - 12	❏
	chapters 13 - 15	❏
	chapters 16 - 18	❏
	chapters 19 - 22	❏

Scripture Memorization   Matthew 16:18 ❏

Cut out Memorization Cards along lines

2 Timothy 3:16

All scripture is given by inspiration of God, and is profitable for doctrine, for reproof, for correction, for instruction in righteousness.: [17] That the man of God may be perfect, thoroughly furnished unto all good works. (KJV)

Romans 16:17

Now I beseech you, brethren, mark them which cause divisions and offences contrary to the doctrine which ye have learned; and avoid them. (KJV)

Romans 10:9

That if thou shalt confess with thy mouth the Lord Jesus, and shalt believe in thine heart that God hath raised him from the dead, thou shalt be saved. [10] For with the heart man believeth unto righteousness; and with the mouth confession is made unto salvation. (KJV)

John 8:31

Then said Jesus to those Jews which believed on him, If ye continue in my word, then are ye my disciples indeed; (KJV)

Speak The Word

I have the Word of God as my doctrine
and I will avoid those
who teach and preach otherwise.

Speak The Word

I am thoroughly furnished
unto all good works,
by the power of God's Word.

Speak The Word

I continue in God's Word,
therefore,
I am a disciple of the Lord.

Speak The Word

I confess with my mouth
that Jesus is Lord, I believe in my heart
that God has raised Him from the dead,
therefore I am saved,
I am a child of God,
I am born again.

Cut out Memorization Cards along lines

Malachi 3:10
Bring ye all the tithes into the storehouse, that there may be meat in mine house, and prove me now herewith, saith the LORD of hosts, if I will not open you the windows of heaven, and pour you out a blessing, that there shall not be room enough to receive it. (KJV)

Acts 1:8
But ye shall receive power, after that the Holy Ghost is come upon you: and ye shall be witnesses unto me both in Jerusalem, and in all Judaea, and in Samaria, and unto the uttermost part of the earth. (KJV)

John 15:7
If ye abide in me, and my words abide in you, ye shall ask what ye will, and it shall be done unto you. (KJV)

John 4:24
God is a Spirit: and they that worship him must worship him in spirit and in truth. (KJV)

Speak The Word

I am empowered by the Holy Spirit
to be a witness of the Lord.
I am a witness; all the time, in every place,
to everyone.

Speak The Word

I worship God in all of my ways,
from the depth of my heart,
in spirit and in truth.

Speak The Word

I pay tithes of all of my income,
therefore the house of the Lord is full
and the windows of heaven are open to me.
God is pouring out abundant blessings into
my life

Speak The Word

As a believer I abide in Christ,
and as an obedient student of the Word,
His words abide in me,
therefore I ask what I will according to His
Word
and it is done unto me.

Psalms 103:2
Bless the LORD, O my soul, and forget not all his benefits:
³ Who forgiveth all thine iniquities; who healeth all thy diseases; (KJV)

Matthew 16:18
And I say also unto thee, That thou art Peter, and upon this rock I will build my church; and the gates of hell shall not prevail against it. (KJV)

Mark 11:23
For verily I say unto you, That whosoever shall say unto this mountain, Be thou removed, and be thou cast into the sea; and shall not dobut in his heart, but shall believe that those things which he saith shall come to pass; he shall have whatsoever he saith.
²⁴ Therefore I say unto you, What things soever ye desire, when ye pray, believe that ye receive them, and ye shall have them. (KJV)

Matthew 3:11
I indeed baptize you with water unto repentance: but he that cometh after me is mightier than I, whose shoes I am not worthy to bear: he shall baptize you with the Holy Ghost, and with fire: (KJV)

Speak The Word

Christ has built His church.
His church will not fail.
Because I am born again,
I am in His church.
Being in His church
all of hell cannot prevail against me.

Speak The Word

Jesus is my baptizer.
He does all things well.
As I submit to Him, I am filled,
and am continually being refilled
with the Spirit.

Speak The Word

I bless the Lord
and remember all His benefits.
He forgives all my sins
and heals all my diseases.

Speak The Word

As God's Word fills my heart,
and I make it the confession of my mouth,
God will cause me to have whatsoever I say.